SCIENCE & STEEPLEFLOWER

Also by Forrest Gander

Poetry
Deeds of Utmost Kindness
Lynchburg
Rush to the Lake

Translations
Mouth to Mouth: Poems by Twelve Contemporary Mexican Women

SCIENCE & STEEPLEFLOWER

FORREST GANDER

A NEW DIRECTIONS BOOK

Grateful acknowledgment is made to the editors and publishers of the following journals in which some of these poems were first published: *American Letters and Commentary, American Poetry Review, Boston Book Review, Colorado Review, Conjunctions, Denver Quarterly, First Intensity, Grand Street, Jacket, Luna, The Southern Review, Sulfur,* and *Volt.* "Duration and Simultaneity" was first published in a program for the Un-terberg Poetry Center at the 92nd St. YMCA in New York. "Deflection Toward the Relative Minor" first appeared in *Outsiders* (Laure-Anne Bosselaar, ed., Milkweed Editions). "Time and the Hour" first appeared in *Verse & Universe: Poems About Science and Mathematics* (Kurt Brown, ed., Milkweed Editions). "Eggplants and Lotus Root" was published as a chapbook by Burning Deck Press, and further thanks is paid to Rosmarie Waldrop for permission to reprint it here.

AUTHOR'S NOTE: I would like to thank The Fund For Poetry for its unexpected sup-port, and the Virginia Center for the Arts for a summer residency amid good com-pany. Thanks also to Bradford Morrow and to Douglas Messerli.

Book and cover design by Erik Rieselbach
Manufactured in the United States of America
New Directions Books are printed on acid-free paper.
First published as a New Directions Paperbook Original in 1998
Published simultaneously in Canada by Penguin Books Canada Limited

Library of Congress Cataloging-in-Publication Data
Gander, Forrest, 1956–
Science and steepleflower / Forrest Gander.
p.   cm. — (New Directions paperbook)
ISBN 0-8112-1381-1 (alk. paper)
I. Title.
PS3557.A47S3 1998
811'.54—dc21   97-36062
                                        CIP

New Directions Books are published for James Laughlin
by New Directions Publishing Corporation
80 Eighth Avenue, New York 10011

FOR KAZUO OHNO

Along the cliffs of these mountains, locked in snow,
Are the tracks of only one. That one is you.
 —Murasaki Shikibu
  (tr. Edward G. Seidensticker)

Contents

I.

And I'll love my distinction: Near or far
He says his science helps him not to look
At hopes so evil-heaven'd as mine are.
　　　　　　　—"The Beginning of the End,"
　　　　　　　Gerard Manley Hopkins

TIME AND THE HOUR

The convulsive incision   tore light
from matter, image   from similitude, black vowels
croaked and flew   from the four-lettered name of God.
In diffuse nebulae,   non-luminous metals shined
in their planets.   The thirty intentions of the shadows
condensed below a brightness   the multitude
of species emitted, and Ras Algethi   glared in Hercules.
So the light came   to contain numbers
and the first   was intoxication
and Giotto was intoxicated   painting Scrovegni,
1306.   Out in the fields—wheat,
cockleburs, jimson—   a farmer stood up his hoe
and when that hoe was standing   on its own shadow,
he knew, and he was certain   that he knew.

DURATION AND SIMULTANEITY

The cicada collapses   its eardrum, blocking out
its own song   or goes deaf

On a lowering   and sad evening,
your presence   answers

Constellations   hold
only the gaze   from another time

I cup them to my face   crushed birch leaves:
extravagance of your washed hair

The stars are coming apart   I myself

        also   after this night

        is night   apart

TO LIVE WITHOUT SOLACE

This is the meaning of the vision:
the body's sawing stride. Before which, before appearance
appeared, god in the glint
unmoving stood like a scarecrow in a garden of cucumbers.
Though, not god. It was without a god's claw-tipped brain,
and unforeseeing. Only: an incisive force. A contraction
and release, a woman's hands around bedposts, and the heavy elements
in clouds of interstellar gas began to cleave

                                    into complex molecules
whose signature and measure were unmistakable.

                                   In lithesome undulation,
the world came true. Warblers adjusted their pitch
by an order of magnitude. The day uprighted,
gleaming with wounds. Sand crunched underfoot and the air
put on a blue cloak embroidered with swallows.
The goat-lipped young men holding hands
felt the throbbing begin, felt it beat into speech, and they called each other
with throaty cluckings and amphetamine
hearts. The headbands tightened
                         around their temples.

When the intensity decreased, seared iron
going ochre from cherry-red, all reached out and touched the flickering
rhythm like horse-buyers and their nostrils flared and they took a piece
of the music between their teeth like meat, deerflies

scrimming their eyes. Still the pulse bowled them over.
Breath and durance ceased.
And the thing went inside them and out again as along a spoke
and they thrashed to remember what it was like.
And the water croaked before a stalking crane.

MOON AND PAGE GHAZAL

Before the neutrinos could interact with matter, they went out.
His voice hardened. The foreplay went out.

Through a pocked sky he dragged her by the rope in her mouth.
She didn't like it. When he opened the door, her stray went out.

To wound him no deeper than to awaken him, she thought.
Under eaves, the buzzing of mud daubers in their piped clay went out.

That could not be his meaning, on two legs walking backward.
But whoever heard her pray went out.

Only a fly responds to a moving hand in thirty milliseconds.
Biting the hole in her lip as each day went out.

They met at the footsteps of the altar, in a groined chamber of salt.
Forever, she said—*flash*—smiling as the bridesmaid went out.

THE CEREMONY OF OPENING THE MOUTH
AND THE EYES

Now, for instance, in the after-storm sheen,
just when you are beginning your sentence leaning
toward me taking a deep breath,
in the merely allowed seeing, the between
dips of the head when horses water, aromatized by sweat,
the air vibrant with mosquitoes, rapt of you,
impregnate with your conversation,

                              even in this exquisite and common
HERE, the strictly expressed, I fall through
our part of the text to the scrim
beyond your word

                    in slow anguilliform movements.
Away AND TOWARD. As eels swim
palindromically. Not receding so much as underdrawn.

                                   Dismissing
your sparked eyes,
the bubble of your morpheme not yet exploding into a thud—

A schizophrenic said, *I heard a voice say: he is conscious of life.*
Soul, multilingual in the same tongue.
And as the orthogonals roll back to a trace
between us, intention comes to be
the dead rose in a vase cloying with leeches. I

                                  open
my finger on the thorn. I hear the black tongues crawling my forearm
called by your voice, your cool matutinal warbling, to enrich

my hearing with another hearing.
                              Because cognition comes only
by contrast. Superimposing on C7
an E-flat 7. So
                              am I
unlocated until the later event requires me.
Smeared between distinct values, I find you here also.
                              You are also here,
the deviation
of an ellipse from the circle, breath stopped
in the circle of your teeth.

Here. Purchasing a clearance,
enclosing our names in a double cartouche. Parting with the known
without division, ahead of time. And all this thrashing
                              in the incandescent,
formless marrow—before the mourning cloak lays one
orange   egg   on   one   bittercress   leaf   next to your
finger. While I wheel toward your awakened face, the waterfall of your word.

FACE

What lasts in thinking is not
So much the way
As its horizon, the plum side
Not facing us but richer
In contingency

                    a lateral
Sheer rock wall
From which hiero-
Glyphs wave what
Lasts comes after
The red flash
The negative
Commemoration outside of
Syntax, human
Recognition turned away
From finally itself

                    to pinions, one seed
Junipers, scree
Blasted like rusty cans
The prehistoric wind blinds
Us with dust a cactus
Spine goes through our shoe
But we are bent
Upon not that

THE FINE-STRUCTURE CONSTANT

When there was no sign of awakened attention, when his blood drained
                                                        to one side,
Who noticed crab spiders dispersing in July air?

Why would the waitress turning chairs onto tables sigh
That at least he had lived like a faucet turned on?

His luck ran out? He didn't have luck. If he decided
He needed cowshit, the cows would become constipated.

A blue forehead vein surfaced when he spoke.
Since when did it take psychology to see
Shyness and pride lour in his eyes?

What did he show us we had not already seen?
He cut his coffee with honeysuckle.

The phone rang once and quit. Why
Did the hair rise on his neck?

Does a white cabbage-butterfly
See the dandelion plume
Caught also in the web,
Or only curved hind-legs drawing from the spinnerets?

In a region where God's purpose chooses not to extend itself,
How is momentum introduced, the weight that turns the scale?

Along the road, houses were dark. Was it moonlight against barbed wire
Or catfish heads hung there, ringing like a bell?

Was he drunk when he screamed
From the top of a pine
That the palms of his hands
Had fallen off of him?

Two monks carrying a burnt lectern
On a two-by-four to the brush arbor. No one recognized them?

Do me a favor, the sheriff advised; keep your eyes
Peeled for wetbacks. They handcuffed him,
Didn't they, when he answered, I
Wouldn't piss in your ear if your brain were on fire.

Just who did he expect would believe he could hear
The floral revelry, as he called it, and the stridulations of ants?

And if no one returns, how do we interpret
The belted kingfisher's rattle-laugh?

A DISSONANCE LEADING TO A MODULATION

Specific words are uttered and specific gestures made
on a particular morning. But the existence of these words
and gestures cannot be accounted for. Outside
the universe, where there is no space, there is not nothing.

                                        Unblinking,

the eyes of a white-throated monitor
shear into friction-heated disks of luminous gas
before we cross the meridian,

                      that ridge

forested on one side and bare
in its rain shadow. By memory not measurement
we distinguish the slip from attention, the hawk

                              riding updrafts five

thousand feet high from a drowned caddis fly
drifting downstream.
To occupy the place religiously, some allowed themselves to spread

                                    outward

like the ring of a rising fish. They only drew in the darkness
behind them. Their distance increased.
For who can become implicate with the brute matter of experience

                                    and still tender

devotion to an invisible claimant? And the seductive desire
for oblivion, and shadings of timbre? As though we could not see,
as though the deceptive, linear clarity of an explorer's map

kept us from seeing
the smudge on the mirror.

                    We say
the streak is an optical artifact or a green-backed firecrown
tonguing nectar from quintral flowers. We say we are somehow rich

                                                    enough

for multiple, even inconsistent accounts. No one comes prepared
for the meaning of the sentence.
Yet we compass. Sometimes. We see.

II.

FIELD GUIDE TO SOUTHERN VIRGINIA

True as the circumference
to its center. Woodscreek Grocery,
Rockbridge County. Twin boys
peer from the front window, cheeks
bulging with fireballs. Sandplum trees
flower in clusters by the levee. She
makes a knot on the inside knob
and ties my arms up
against the door. Williamsburg green.
With a touch as faint as a watermark.
Tracing cephalon, pygidium, glabella.

Swayback, through freshly cut stalks,
stalks the yellow cat. Can you smell
where analyses end, the orchard
oriole begins? Slap her breasts lightly
to see them quiver. Delighting in this.
Desiccation cracks and plant debris
throughout the interval. In the Black-
water River, fishnets float
from a tupelo's spongy root
chopped into corks. There may be sprawling
precursors, descendent clades there are none.

The gambit declined was less
promising. So the flock of crows
slaughtered all sixty lambs. Toward the east, red
and yellow colors prevail.
Praying at the graveside,
holding forth the palm of his hand
as a symbol of God's book.
For the entirety of the Ordovician.
With termites, Mrs. Elsinore explained,
as with the afterlife, remember:
there are two sides to the floor. A verb
for inserting and retrieving
green olives with the tongue. From
the scissure of your thighs.

In addition, the trilobites
were tectonically deformed. Snap-on
tools glinting from magenta
loosestrife, the air sultry
with creosote and cicadas.
You made me to lie down in a peri-Gondwanan back-arc basin.
Roses of wave ripples and gutter casts.
Your sex hidden by goat's beard.
Laminations in the sediment. All
preserved as internal molds
in a soft lilac shale.

Egrets picketing the spines of cattle in fields edged
with common tansy. Flowers my father gathered
for my mother to chew. To induce abortion. A common,
cosmopolitan agnostoid lithofacies naked in the foothills. I love
the character of your intelligence, its cast as well as pitch.
Border wide without marginal spines. At high angles
to the inferred shoreline.

It is the thin flute of the clavicles, each rain-pit
above them. The hypothesis of flexural loading. Aureoles
pink as steepleflower. One particular day, four hundred
million years ago, the mud stiffened
and held the stroke of waves. Orbital motion.
Raking leaves from the raspberries, you
uncover a nest of spring salamanders.

III.

EXHAUSTIBLE APPEARANCE

Around the burning barn, stationary objects seem to stream.

Scrub brush, twigs in sinople dirt, dry weeds,

puffballs among scattered breccia and chert.

Grey barn burning in the grey eye of the afternoon.

The solid given upward, hemorrhaging into air, the vista

tinged Merthiolate and twisted inside the barn, a dense ball of smoke

like a black sock

        stuffed in a shoe.

                We breathe carbonized splinters, our shirts beating

to exploding planks, holding barely within ourselves the felt

quality of redness, whoosh, heat. Roof gone, walls seared

down to the single argent window gleaming…

        And here, to keep the whole visual image from slipping across

                           the retina,

away, we focus upon the window—

        which does not reflect any panorama we see

        which does not reveal the penetralia

        which neither contributes nor borrows any color

from the chromatic blaze

        which, though gravity always tugged the glass down

through itself, melts quickly now.

Nothing in the window of the world beside it the world within it the
world we can see around, beyond it.

The window catches light from another world altogether,
one behind us, one we cannot see, the world from which we have come
clomping across the desert from a road which is a dashed trace
on a map.

It is a moteless clarity behind us.

Not a mature representation of imagined form.
Not a clot of flies at the edge of a cow's eye. Not tadpoles wriggling
                                                    in the mud of a
tractor tread. Not a broken bootlace.

But when we turn, like a piece of music at the andante,
the landscape resumes. The barn fallen inside itself.

THE ARK UPON HIS SHOULDERS

My husband did all this.   We used to live

in a rambling kind of house   with gossipy verandas.

Then he bought a stove, an iron stove   with a reservoir to it.

He always insisted it was bad luck   to come in that door

and go out the other. It's bad luck   to pay back salt

if you borrow it.   To the day he died

he smelled   pulled up from the dirt. He worked

the Norfolk Southern forty years   walking on top

of freight trains. I've seen him   up there

and the wind just blowing—   you could see the wind

blowing his clothes.

       Our second house   he built it.

Cut me a yard broom   from dogwood bushes,

tied in three places. Hogs   squealed under the floorboards

in winter—you could see one   through the cracks.

He had something he said   to hush them.

Come up the porch steps   arms full of lightwood.

In those days   we drank good old cool water

out of the well—cool and   put some syrup in it

and stir it up   and drink it right along

with our dinner. The summers were   so hot you saw

little devils   twizzling out in front of you.

He called them   lazy jacks. It was the heat.

Listen at that bird,   he'd say. It's telling us,

Love one another. He caught   a ride back

from town with seeds and a hoop   of greasy cheese and crackers
                   and
sardines and light   bread. He carried that umbrella
over me and I   would have his hat walking to church.
We lost the first one.   The midwife came late, she used dirt-
dauber tea for my pains.   He tried telling me
it wasn't any death owl, it was a ordinary hoot owl outside
the house. But I tied a knot   in my sheet
so it wouldn't quiver.   I was in such trouble,
he petted me a lot. Three days   labor he attended me
how a dragonfly hovers   over water in the clear sun.
The next year we had a beautiful girl baby, Ruthie.
Ruthie, after my mother.   Towards the end,
he was a bit thick-listed.   I never yelled though, he read
                 my lips.

When the katydid   chirps, I miss him
saying there'll be forty days until frost.   Ones who were in
                 trouble
they always   sought him out. Listen
at that bird, he'd say.
The things he knew how to do he did them.

EDGE-LIT SCENE

Turns to her, then,   from the northern
oriole taking a dust   bath. It is her voice
unseats him. Years   it will take
    to thread himself back   into the dull wood.

Two spider bikes lean   against the Dairy Dream,
their shadows, toward evening,   an aftertenderness
    she sees and aches.

With children, they grow   more involved,
    more isolate,   like grazing animals, vaguely
aware of the other.

And something small slips   from them, murmur rising
above a crowd's silence   during the performance.

It is their performance. Like hens they fill   rooms with their voices
not because the egg,   in passing out, hurts them.
Because the place has been made   empty within.

When they tithe their attention,   the thing itself
is incomprehensible. They think   they have swallowed
    stones for each other. They think   they are blocked
    by their sacrifices,   suffocating

in a dark shaft.   Who can say
   they will hit again   that gorgeous galena ore
which is emotion,   the fact of emotion?

ESCAPED TREES OF LYNCHBURG

Mostly, they live disagreeably   amid volleys of far-off barking
and a chalk lake, spring-fed,   clear. Watercress and wild
celery in the current   undulate. Trees, the central figures
of their own originality,   come bare down the slope
to bathe.   Sudden raptus in the land,
arborescing.   The poplar
and its reflection   are disturbing, like twins.

The trees live disagreeably,   secreting
chemicals that attract   parasitic wasps
when caterpillars start   to strip the leaves.
February sap rose   from woodpecker holes.
Surreptitiously deft,   willows speed in their lingering,
all together and insolent,   acoustic nodes on their branches
sough a neuter language.

Each topos is seeded   by a loop of tendril.
In mud around the lake   horsefly larvae, partly buried,
pierce the bellies of young toads,   suck them dry. The present
is the unknown, a development   without resemblance. A small
inflorescence of blue   mist from stills
precarious on upward slopes   will condense the cow-smell
and hold it to the hills   like a shadow cast in space.

Winter tits hovered,   dipped their beaks into sap
at the icicle's tip.   The land arborescing, that secret
neuter language,   and no one to decipher
the concealed from the given.

MARGINAL LUMINOSITY

End of the 18th century: the sun begins, only
then, to assume its modern appearance,
its early angular momentum
carried off by magnetic winds. Your snood
and thin skirt at Playa Azul
are bucked away in the surf. And the dog-
day locust and glowworm
open their spiracles to breathe. Not choice
but annunciation. A cleaved mica leaf,
the smoothest surface known. But your eyes
as I near, and their brightness increasing,
the sublime scent of warmth
at your throat. Endlessly, in a room
raucous with caged birds, Uccello drew
polyhedrons in foreshortening.
Not expression, but recognition. Darkness rises
through beer foam. Puddles of cow-flux
under the juniper. After our first
intimacy, we wasted years
deploying the hedgehog formation
instead of dissolving the center pawns. First frost
wipes out mosquitoes and the blackflies
swarm in earnest. With what instrument do we measure
the integrity of our minds

filled with each other? We who, one evening, will open the door
to a delicate boy whose torch burns upside down.
We who can hear at this distance beetle nymphs
scurrying on the floor of the poultry run.

SINISTER

As if a distinction might be drawn at the edge of a continuum.
As if this might shake us by the teeth.

You know that vagrant at hogkilling time he goes
farm to farm collecting dried bladders.
This is the bone he stuck in your gate.

As if the salted beer foam and boiled egg were
repercussions of our own feeling,
as if the barn swallows told us nothing.

He burns a scent into his clothes
to cover the hogstink, he chews on cloves.

As if this sentence were a cliff
and a witness, that dry birdnote its postulate.

Shows up at The Triangle one Saturday a month,
sits across from the mirror.

As if transformation came
from the isomorphic pressure
of close attention. As if, tenting his fingers,
his beauty were purified by restraint.

Outside the package store, with that Polaroid
you gave me, I took his photograph.
I've had these sooty paw prints under my eyes,
he said, *since time out of mind.*

As if the sadness of pictures
had to do with our exclusion,
even from those in which we appear.

As though our theories unfit us for wholeness,
and the surfaces were crazed,
and there were not time
to recover the yolk of ourselves.

He admired his likeness. *My wife's blind,*
he told me. *Last night in the yard,*
fireflies come out. Fireflies, I said.
She nodded yes. Then I heard, far off,
what she heard, horseshoes clanging.

IV.

It may be that universal history is the history of the different intonations given a handful of metaphors.

—Jorge Luis Borges

THE HISTORY OF VENERATION

At which time, partly,

she recovered

herself. Her memory, as if traced from the underdrawing,
came back. Begged us to take her home. Eyes welling
as though she had done something wrong. *Please give me one more*

chance. And then

the sounds stopped
coming from her mouth and she was a pantomime of grief.

Shriveled to this,

who had midwived calves and horses, who—
in one hour of one day—stood back to back with her husband, larding

her right arm,

a blistering June, and plunging it into the dry friable vagina to push

back

the body of a fetus

while he rooted for the foreleg, who corded the upper, straightened limb

and head

and rotated the body searching out
the missing leg, who blindly slid her hand—one hour, one day—over

the brim

of pelvis and forehead probing for a nose, feeling for the mouth
until its muzzle rested in the palm of her hand

so the jaw would not drop

open and sharp teeth cut the womb's floor.

Each convulsive NOW, a locus of experience
to which no one returns because the way rushes close and seals.

                                                Behind her,

the past whelms, a humid space
she had, momentarily, displaced. What little, finally, etc.
Lives we don't know. A night blooming cereus
on the windowsill, a radio—scratch music
throbbing left and right of the station where she set the dial. Closer
and closer. We sit like demi-puppets
arrayed around her bed not looking at each other. Stand, one by one,
kiss her goodbye, one by one.

THE HISTORY OF DOMESTICITY

I.
Bullfrog bray
No sleep hot
Under sheet
To drink less
Lie wrong love's
Spot engriefed
A wake in
Skirling brief
Birdsong her
Dream wail soft
Wife as soot
I rake in
Knee crooked
Bare skin there
And foot say
Love to hair
Hours accrue
Taking hours
To

II.

The farther south the better
Light comes on
Slantwise through thin
Shiver drift the light
Breath, far south tearing
Page startled
Early light
Delivers us
Singeing hair and
Rises in the looking
Bare a page circumscribed
Attention there-
Fore language, the
Wind starts
Its currency the burned
Volant shadow
Graving
The small sleeping child

THE HISTORY OF MANIFEST DESTINY

And as they brought no
Thing to barter, no Otter
Skins, we slew the lot—
Land in view yet
Haze over it—
They were copperish
But clean,
No greasy paint
About their faces an ochre
Wind bore us favor
N22 W5 we had it
Chiefly calm

In wild blossom balm
On a tree
We found the skeleton of a child
Wrapt carefully
In bark cloth
And sudden as we pokd it
A brood of mice pourd out
But what
So dazzld our eyes
Grew everywhere nearby,
A species of Valerian
With tiny reddish flowers

So at the Meridian hour
Stood we in for shore
Tryd Soundings
Had no ground— our
Legs toes hands gone weak
From hunger,
Our faces dark, hazelly—
And grave the mountains broke
Unto verdant pasturage
With wood and winding valleys
Capable, we wagerd,
Of the highest state of improvement
By English brace and plow

In our way, vast flights of fowl—
Auks Divers Ducks Wild Geese—
So exceeding shy our sportsmen were
At loss to show their art
Mistook spoutings of whales
In such a hazy horizon
To be strange vessels
Under sail
Brought to and fired
Our leeward guns

The ship found crank, 20 tons
Of shingle ballast we got
On board a place cald Indian
Rock, natives
Scudding into the woods
Rods of smoking clams,
Bearskins and dried Salmon
They left for us behind

Two men approachd made signs
Their bows and arrows
An inferior sort they spoke
A clattery jargon
Stout fellows pittd
With smallpox each
Destitute
Of an eye, tied one up
Instructd the other
In quarter hour
To return
With Otter Skins

For the infidel's sins
The black head
Of our prisoner

Who repeatd one
Constant word
We skewerd
Upright
On a pole and dind
Beside this point
Resumd our course
Mortified to find
A fresh Northerly breeze
Right in our teeth

A seaman lowerd a wreath
Of trinkets to the canoe
That with Otter Skins came off for us
Shewing neither dread
Nor vestige of apprehension
Yet with menacing signs
Uttering Poo Poo
By which was meant our muskets
They wantd mainly copper
Their Otter Skins hauld up
Our Captain triald their luck
Ballast was dropt through their crafts
Which sank

By and by
A bird flew past
Much resembling a duck

THE HISTORY OF A WOBBLING AXIS

Not yet, however, dipping her tongue into the holy-water stoup
for the sheer ass of it. Brought up chewing, she claims,
the stems of African violets or, alternately,
nursed by blacksnakes on honey.

Born as though for the last time on the last day
for a bird nest contest, her hair
perfumed with Hatsune incense, big toenail
banged loose, the fire dog twisting wildly on its back

in the grass in a salmagundi of ants. Become implicate then
with a man who emptied the decanter of himself while she was there
to see phosphenic patterns adrift, fading behind his eyes.
                                        And not able
to step over the shattered robin's egg, going
the long way out of the garden. She bears exacting witness,

urine stains on all four hubcaps, and so
like blonde crickets under the well cover, endlessly curious
about bite-proven metal and such dark matter
as dominates the halo of spiral star clusters
or a wall behind which something is said
to be happening. Through the immediate and strictly mediate,
                                        on the porch,
heaping greenbeans onto newspaper,

finds a way for herself like air in a bagpipe. Lightly,
furling black sails.

ORIENTATION ROSES, A HISTORY

I. *SELECT ENERGY. Apply conductive paste to paddles. Place paddles on chest—apply firm pressure.*

1996

A telephone
swinging on its cord in the rain outside Penn Station. Alone,

sitting in the taxi, mopping hair back, dress shoes
submersed in a pool of black

water. Tumultuous predawn wind. A few figures borne down
Avenue D. Glimpse into the alley. A Miocene ape with-
draws into darkness. Car horn.

Someone sweeping the hall with a newspaper under one shoe,
back and forth past the door,
back, pause, and forth.

Agreeing to share the clanging radiator, tiny room,
with a stranger from Spain. The swabbed toilets
spew into the hall
their aseptic, grape perfume.

From the warm terminal,
caught in a peristaltic convulsion of crowd

through the corridor, past shops, up the escalator and released
into the raw loud afternoon, its yellow line of taxis.
Crossing the street
       tentatively toward Peep

World. Milky trails drip
below the hole between stalls.
Drizzle. On the 5 A.M. subway grate,
upside-down, between cars and fenced gingkoes,
a dozen umbrellas at large
in the deserted street, inexplicably discarded.

The iron cellar-doors in the sidewalk trampoline under foot.
Don't pet her—the woman in furs—*she's mean.*

Transfixed in the stifling heat by the Spaniard
whose bulging purple underwear throbs
and begins to darken in his sleep.

II.   CHARGE. Push charge button on apex paddle. Wait for ready tone.

1967

The groaning and gnatting of early, sudden dark.

Glimpse in the headlights: an arm
distended from the semi's window,
burst of orange sparks

on the road. Muddying
for channel cats with a gig and a hoe.

Greasy handprints, face-level on the wall
over the filling station's urinal. Young
chokeberry trees lean toward

a stained screen at the abandoned drive-in.
Hidden, watching, afraid to cough. It takes all of them
to get her panties off.

A long steaming tongue of blue asphalt
beside the rice field. The prison work crew sitting
above the culvert, laughing, passing chew.

Palms up for communion
wafer, embarrassed by the fart.

Stumbling in the woods over the remnants of a long
stone wall white as backbone

under dead leaves. Again, the cow
plops a foot in the bucket. Outraged, leaping from the stool
to dump the milk on her head.

From the garage's creosote shadow, looking out
mesmerized, into the maw of day,
wrenches glint in the driveway.

Three-legged beagle racing the pickup, an insane
look of joy in its face.

*III. DISCHARGE. STAND CLEAR OF PATIENT. Press both paddle dis-
charge buttons simultaneously.*

V.

EGGPLANTS AND LOTUS ROOT

tea scripture

GEOMETRIC LOSSES

or her hair. Its rain. Her face juts out from.
Winter rooms of electricity, her hair lifts. The rug
coarse as hog stubble. Musk in her hair. Held down
by the neck. Or in. At once recognizable, near-burning.
White mole to the right of her coccyx, those
hairs. Inside of her ears is sweating. A sense of
duration spilt across the pillow. Vague and specific like.
An analogy undislodgeable. Pubic hair under tongue.
Words spoken into

VIOLENCE'S NARRATIVE CONTINUED

Dead of winter barechested in the Green Forest
bar. Each wears a cap, roughly half "backwards." Frog-
eyed son of a bitch. Claimed his hound was Death. On
snakes. Want to put it in their pocket and walk around
with it. Floor's tongue and clotted groove. Tiny hexes
of dirt from their Redwings. At the window, among neon
letters, with no arms, stands the reverend. Admonition's
gargoyle. Glass fogs out his face. Hours pass. Then. Who
bursts in holding one shoe. One foot in a paper bag.

MEDITATIVE

When the schoolbus, lights
flashing, confronts the howling ambulance—
which pauses?

"There is a ruttish
perfume, proposition
inexpressible
in a human language,"
begins Death's phosphorous
voice, a little
in drag.

Marbled evening sky over.

Rutilant.

monitory

GEOMETRIC LOSSES

full suddenly. "Still through the hawthorn blows
the cold wind." What I wanted to say was her hair. At the
dressing stand or lies she made. Mouths in a glass. With
her hair let down. Among the cattails redwings. That I
could feel how sharper than the cold wind was. Undone
like an illumination. The mornings it happened. Echo.
Simultaneously. Disturb the black mud of the ferruginous
mud of. The poem. Such as torture, a simple fact. Having
nothing to do with. *Departure, its logarithms of description*

VIOLENCE'S NARRATIVE CONTINUED

The upper gate rail's sticky green surface—
momentarily gripped—was nearly invisible under
a dense layer of dead and dying insects caught to
the paint, like a pale arm taken over by black moles.
This, he vaulted this. Approaching the mansion,
couldn't stop imagining how she would look
pregnant, his brain an acre of hissing grass. A cold
summer's 2 A.M. The ocean's slant eye closing and
closing in sand. Someone forgot to turn off the lawn
sprinkler. The wind shifted, wet him. Froth on the tips
of her breasts, from deep sleep sits up sits up and stares,
the monophthong of the jimmied back door captured
by, lost to receding dream. The man he was the man
who the man who. Invoking room set apart by red ribbon.

MEDITATIVE

It is often possible
to take up a point of view—
crude palimpsest of memory and sensation—
other than one's own
as a dog might piss on a horse's leg.

Caught by her longish
hair she flew around the room
attached to the huge pulley belt.

And is passed away
into the adjoining fringe
and selvage of this fragment.
But the clarity
of the word "is"
is a deception.
How many times

have you descended?
Which the largest bale
you will metabolize?

a macula of light

GEOMETRIC LOSSES

never so much as. An oblique angle. Primitive
oath, blood azimuth. Her light cholera and one hundred
more questions. The dreamt achievement, an enscorpioned
audience. In the furrow weeds. Then double-combs her
hair. Pallbearer's vintage. When the bird begins alone
the light. Its steady fillip into drain. Similarly but later,
directed against telephone pole, its pizzle's hard pulse.
Absence propped in her chair to preach. Critical orchestra.
Low man among stinging arachnids grips the spade. *Dawn's*
on him

VIOLENCE'S NARRATIVE CONTINUED

Didn't he have a loincloth over his gentiles. And
Goody's Headache Powder. Objects in mirror are moroser
than they appear. Disconnected last thoughts. Between
the white center lanes a large red stain. Ascension Parish.
In the shaggy tree lodges one hubcap. The radio song finished.
Without the driver. I Attend Gloryland Baptist Church bum-
persticker. Visible. On the bumper. Impaled on the bridge
rail. Remember, someone had joked, rubber-side down. In
humid air the wheels each freely spinning. Who's going
to tell?

MEDITATIVE

A dog manages to catch its own tail. At first
the traveler laughs, but then shouts and weeps.
No news will ever be obtained regarding that
about to be lost.

Rain for forty days. Surrounded by mountains.
When it brims, the water has raised him to the
peak.

The responses to death are sometimes funny.
A man opens his wrist without drawing blood;
a woman opens a book with nothing inside.

close to water

GEOMETRIC LOSSES

some form retains. Hair at aureole. I of. Sperm.
She wipes her cleavage. How would you sit full of news
on my lap, facing. Guillotines raised over dark eyes. Crossed
a bare common. We, surrounded by neglect. Or drunk,
the bridgelights watery, bridgelights sputtering in the river's
mouth. Curious syntaxes as intimate. Menstrual flow, the
moon from Guanajuato, the pock-faced dead clutching their
genitals, gaping. *To mean anything*

VIOLENCE'S NARRATIVE CONTINUED

"But don't they leak," he asked the Harley dealer.
"They don't leak they leave their mark."
Chirping so loudly. He woke. Continued when
he mentioned this. The phone rang reminding him
of the call he had forgotten to make. Which now could
not be made for the line was busy. Etc. Flowing from eyes
nose mouth tears. Night birds' dialog: one note bent up
like an eyelash and the other double-combing her ferruginous
hair, tsk tsk tsk tsk. Sudden desire to see a woman's pubic
triangle where there was no such desire a moment before.

MEDITATIVE

Strange
that we come
to worship

silence as an aesthetic
activity, a gift,
that we draw it

to the heart of our spiritual zone
let silence ripen
there with its absences
of gesture in the ungulate night,
silence's anniversary, of our penetration.

moon in the afternoon

GEOMETRIC LOSSES

harshed her. Lied she was thick-skinned as a
gator. One of which was. Too longish for the painter's.
Nor—and also sibilantly curved—a brush bristle. Imbed-
ded suchwise in the wall under a smoothed surface.
Anaconda beneath thinly crusted water. Otherwise a
merely enacted principle. She left several hairs. Their
curved flanks quivering, their necks like beaches, an un-
bearable pungence speaking. *But equally non-indicative
of any direction shy of loss*

VIOLENCE'S NARRATIVE CONTINUED

People who did things with their lives. To his eyes
they brought tears. Cardinal in bamboo. His arms
thrown out then sneezes. Morning, more sneezes, sticky
taste. Answers to ding-dong. Seeing the horrible rubber
mask touches his heart. Reads aloud every visible sign
from hearse window. The whole trip. As though illuminations.
How the tea grew bitter. Hank Williams you wrote my life.
Lump in his pants at her funeral. Drizzle. To armless preacher
is coffee served. The gate itself a hell. Open
graves begin to steam. Barking for Bank Patrons Only.
In the summer of Elvis sightings. No shoulder.
A head.

MEDITATIVE

Out from the ordeal
came silence.
Substituted for intention,
thunderstruck by a tongue.
Otherworldly relief

abolishes sthenic sobbing,
rhythmic heaves, wind-whipped
funeral banners. All the less
strange since it is death
who constructs silence,
who climbs into silence
by her longish hair.

coda

and the birds: canthi loosed at a distance. Aqua-
marine backdrop, scratched out several. All symbols
buried in the sand. Nor a cardinal's color nor point, so
only smooth and hush come clear. Unfocused and as if
winked upon. Where the wind, dehiscing sand, does not
omit. In a synoptic way, surrounded: already the eye
whose perceptible tearing: "how the rain swung from
the rims of." Even if it is possible to remain noncommittal
about an endpoint. Winter, thumbprint of black birds
smudged across windshield, in a premature language.
An ocean

VI.

DEFLECTION TOWARD THE RELATIVE MINOR

They were partakers of a strange taste.　　　　At the hour when
Everyone looks for　　　　the passage to his own door
They went at large like　　　　horses. His foot
Wore the steps to her porch.　　　　They were often seen together
Under a dwarf chestnut.　　　　It was said
She had fastened a pin in his walls.　　　　It was said
He had given her his portion,　　　　the firstfruits, and the
Trespass offering,　　　　and the gift of shoulders. His spirit
Was greatly set on fire.

So with grum sentences,　　　　we reproached the pair,
Declaring three similitudes,　　　　showing them their error and
The moth. Explaining　　　　how times wax
Old, they should　　　　suffer straight things, draw in
The common air.

Secretly we prepared　　　　a time to examine him
With despitefulness, to fill　　　　all the places of her joy
With her torn hair.　　　　With resin, pitch, tow,
And small wood we stoked the oven.　　　　But when we came
To arrest them　　　　we were astonished.

Like the keel's trace　　　　in the waves, they were not there.
They were gone together　　　　over the wall into the wilderness

And no one of us followed   but wrote down their names
And buried the paper   in the evening ground when the bell
Sounded for prayer.

ANNIVERSARY

Not to be known always by my wounds,
I buried melancholy's larvae

And cleaved the air behind you.
Myself I gathered

Like the middle dusk
To the black tulips of your nipples.

For seven days we shut the door,
We scoured the room with birds' blood.

And for a little while
In the hollow where your throat rose

From between your splendid clavicles,
Our only rival was music,

The piano of bonewhiteness.
Nor did the light subside,

But deepeningly contracted.
The rawness of the looking.

The quiver.

KNIFE ON A PLATE

If there is any relief from it, any slippage—though wait
while the phalanx of children streaks across the basketball court,

                                              bending

to pick up an eraser at the foul line, and rushes back
to the squealing, eruptive start.
                      Colorful wicks
flickering in the afternoon. My boy
is on fire all summer and losing
his extravagant high voice.
Earth's mantle scatters beneath him.
                       Look where he stands casually leashed
to the greyhound beside the hydrant, a royalty
of self-absorption, yanking the dog before she's through,

               yanking her into the literal present, an uplift
between intention and accommodation,
where hours have yet to be rendered
into days into weeks into months with names
like January and February scrawled into a Daytimer,
into circumscribed feelings.

               The fact of the tag turned out
from the neck of his pajamas attaches itself to me like a burr. The

                                         audacious

originality of the ordinary
sometimes suggests an opening,

and to enter is to hear the measure
not of nostalgia but nearness—that fetching
lack of doubt and perspective, a world
                                zoomed-in close
enough to count black ants
under dog-stunted spirea.
                                Before
capillaries reknot in the eyes, before the dishrag
hanging from a ring on the cabinet door
under the sink is too badly sullied,
the brightest dark and the darkest dark
open huge their mouths. There is a disturbance like a kiss
through which cognition disappears.

As always, I am sitting in this silent room alone,
or I am reading to my son, propped against the headboard.
A donkey finds a magic pebble. The referents
                                for the story's terms
are a function of the story itself,
and the boy knows there is no one world
we approach by approximations.

                Only *choose* and *choose* and *choose*
cracks over us. I jolt awake—
but no time has passed: I am turning the page

with one hand. I am

fingering the boy's unwashed hair.

DEEP ELM

     And then not

even

         face pale and

tragical

        let together   fall

               shirt

    her eyes

Shaving   smells

              behind the ear

       cream,   his mouth

   multiplying

       her cells, fingers

    the seam

of his scrotum

       no relief

       Through her

  soft arms

       there

persimmon, raw

and Silurian

       rain, nameless

    in waves

LANDSCAPE WITH A MAN BEING KILLED BY A SNAKE

Two catfish lock mouths and wrestle
>The marriage fines itself down

You were meant to be blind, she had said,
>That God gave you such hands

He was thinking it was like heat
>Lost to friction in a gear chain

In the freshly darkening evening
>She climbed the cedar to witness

A school of elephant-nosed fish
>Pour tidally from one galaxy to another

Her vision and her grief consubstantial
>He read her perfume's label furtively

Roses, sandalum, and ambergris
>But ivy breaking through window casements

In the cellar, in the reflux of mere circumstance,
>Yellowed— as though the air were poisoned

He came to think only his shouting
>Could ripple the dead, level surface

Because the electric field diminishes
>With the inverse cube of distance

She must have been close to stun him
>Vaguely, wetting the dildo in her mouth

A quel remir contral lums de la lampa
>They went on sleeping in the same bed

And in the luminous runnels of her dream
>He hunted for orange and fly agaric

Her arm bending from the pillow toward the west
                    A shaft of bituminous despair
So nine books of Herodotus' dire *History*
                    Begin with a lover commending
Recklessly the beloved's body

GARMENT OF LIGHT

For two figures preserved at Pompeii

Before the hand stretches out to intensify time's discipline,
it accumulates a thickness, accretionary lapilli.
Horseshoe-shaped calderas gape toward the sea.
                              The bridge begins
as an open chord. In the mountains, falls
are magmatic and subtle.
He does not know where to guide her eyes.

Before gigantic blocks shift
and transform into avalanche, before swifts mute
warm dung in their eyes:
small phreatomagnetic or scoriaceous or small
phreatic explosions, heavy ashfall and darkness for several days.

Where does she hide, now, his nervous, strange exhilaration?
When 3 is the tertiary slope and 6 is the crater rim?
                              How do they go on
chewing words like crickets, if 8
is the landslide, and 10 is the town?
What will their children find to weigh the fire in?

At the tension beyond the opening, they unwrap their secret
voices of fine, bluish-grey pumice shards.

They, known now as consecutive numbers, following
each other to an extreme inner distance.

If lava were not derived of exigence,
the scarp might reveal a parasitic cone.
But volcanic glass hisses forth
carrying free plagioclase crystals. In quiet fumarolic
emissions, the glow faces their faces. Look,
they have scrawled
into the hatched tephra a word
half-obscured by mud
under which they lie. Our days
come tagged to that foreign
inscription, a delicate, enharmonic reply.

Notes

In "The Ceremony of Opening the Mouth and the Eyes," the line, "A schizophrenic said 'I heard a voice say: he is conscious of life'" is quoted from David Cooper's *The Language of Madness* in *A Thousand Plateaus* by Gilles Deleuze and Felix Guattari (University of Minnesota, 1987).

"Face" was written for Arthur Sze.

"Field Guide to Southern Virginia" is for Sally Mann and Larry Mann.

"Exhaustible Appearance" and "Escaped Trees of Lynchburg" were written as responses to photographs by Denny Moers.

Some of the material in "The Ark Upon His Shoulders" is derived, though substantially altered, from the wonderful book *You May Plow Here, The Narration of Sara Brooks* (Norton, 1985).

"Sinister" is for Deborah Luster.

"The History of Manifest Destiny" is inspired by *Archibald Menzie's Journal of Vancouver's Voyage,* April to October 1792.

The structure of "Orientation Roses, a History" is related to the observation that certain diseases—such as alcoholism—and traumas tend to devour memories in reverse order to their acquisition.

"Deflection Toward the Relative Minor" is for Jock O'Hazeldean, of Sir Walter Scott's poem.

"Landscape With a Man Being Killed by a Snake," is for Donald Revell. The title is taken from the unforgettable painting by Nicolas Poussin.

Thanks to the Geology Department at The College of William and Mary. Thanks also to the John Carter Brown Library at Brown University and The Valentine Museum in Richmond, Virginia. A small CAFR grant from Providence College in 1996 was especially helpful to me as I was writing "Field Guide to Southern Virginia."